Roots

(Or, This May Be Where I Came From)

poems by

Lissette Lendeborg

Finishing Line Press
Georgetown, Kentucky

Roots

(Or, This May Be Where I Came From)

Copyright © 2021 by Lissette Lendeborg
ISBN 978-1-64662-414-0 First Edition
All rights reserved under International and Pan-American Copyright Conventions.
No part of this book may be reproduced in any manner whatsoever without written permission from the publisher, except in the case of brief quotations embodied in critical articles and reviews.

ACKNOWLEDGMENTS

Caution to the Wind has previously been published by *Austin International's Di-Verse-City Youth Anthology*.

Publisher: Leah Huete de Maines
Editor: Christen Kincaid
Cover Art and Design: Ty Davis, "Duality"
Author Photo: Lythal LLC, Kevin Vasquez

Order online: www.finishinglinepress.com
also available on amazon.com

Author inquiries and mail orders:
Finishing Line Press
PO Box 1626
Georgetown, Kentucky 40324
USA

Table of Contents

Where the Lakes Make the City 1

Caution to the Wind 2

Revisiting Old Territories 3

Questions to Ask After Midnight 4

Try to Understand 5

Beautiful Interactions 6

On Killing a Lover 7

Screaming Sparks to Flame 8

An Appeal to the Highest Court 9

Crystallized Steps 10

The Ghost on the Water 11

Looking Down from a Cloud 12

When the Beach Aligns with Us 13

Bargaining In My Sleep 14

Filter 15

In the Letter I Wrote to You 16

Long Nights 17

Engraved Backs 18

How to Not Wake Up 19

This Identity 20

"Hello? Anybody There?" 21

Coming to Terms with Letting Go 22

Looking Back on Second Chances 23

Portioned Kisses 24

Florida's Skin 25

Frozen in the Past 26

Where the Lakes Make the City

Since I could crawl,
familiar streets appeared
to look back at me.

I know their roots,
witnessed their conception.
Forged routes

to the hub of *cafecitos*
and *pastelitos*.
Buzzing bakeries bouncing

off Cuban tongues.
Together we indulge guava
and cheese.

Pieces of home embedded in
our taste buds.

Caution to the Wind

I have driven with my eyes closed.
It allows me to listen for red lights, and
feel desperate horns tremble my leather seat.

My grip loosens and I break away
from the burden of control.
With both hands above my head,

the wind wrestles with my fingertips.
Perspective shifts on a revolving focal point.
Driving upside down, my hair gets

tangled in my seat belt.
Fogged mirrors and unbuckled fears
grant access for

unconfined gears and rusted engines.
Refusal disrupts the alignment of my bones.
I lock my knees on acceleration.

Revisiting Old Territories

Rough backs and painted canvas skies.
We watched the stars drip.

I took rocks like guilt and shame,
so you could gaze from comfort.

Swallowing dust to shield your eyes,
so that, one day, you'd reimagine

lost love when you looked at me.
Chipped paint rains on me,

I was unable to keep you
from tarnished memories.

Questions to Ask After Midnight

Where do the clouds go?
The sun takes deep breaths
and rids the sky of its dust.
They drift off to other worlds.

Are the waves angry?
In envy they crave companionship,
and attempt to boast for bystanders.
They wish to be filled,
to take back from the shore.

Why am I in so much pain?
At the brink of greatness,
there are barriers.

What if the clouds don't come back?
Rejoice under settled air,
but mourn with the lonely breeze.
Be mindful of forgotten rain.

Why can't I be a cloud?
Rejoice beside peace.
Accept that you are not far off.

Try to Understand

If I drop my petitions
I trust that you will catch them.
Keep an eye out for what resembles
me yearning for your patience.

When you decide to wander off,
in search of me, I'll be
begging for a fragment of empathy.

Please don't mistake my curious
hands for a pit of donation.
Try to pay me in words of
sentiment, although
I reject foreign love.

Beautiful Interactions

Blemishes on soft skin
drown rugged partners
in salted fragrances
and heavy breathing.

They stroll along silent streams,
on cotton paths of secure
and mutual pursuits.

Laughs like wind chimes,
deep stares like lost coins
in fountains. The subtle shush
of welcoming waves
compose melodic silence.

On Killing a Lover

You do not fail to inject me
with this lover's bane,

words frozen and spiked.
Force fed; pushed through

my barrier of hope and illusions.
Stitch my broken bones with your

poison drenched needle and thread.
Patch my nostalgia with your distant voice.

Silence my once spared heart,
and don't miss.

Screaming Sparks to Flame

Sounds of a tortured self
muffle through gripped lips and clenched teeth.
They resonate to past versions of me.
A naïve existence that threw lights
into the depths of tunnels.

I set my sleeves on fire in a tomb,
left to my own devices. My sleeves crisp,
and catch fire to my chest. Beating hearts
and stamping palms do not suffice in settling out sparks.
Failed attempts leave me scorching.

An Appeal to the Highest Court

To drown out the wailing night,
I pray aloud—hoping that when my tongues
float their way through the floodgates
my shoulders will cling to them.

Hanging from the sky I will inhale
the air of hymns (enough to sustain me).

Amen, and I wake in a bed of quicksand,
(of the many that I make)
frantic attempts at freedom:

"Take me, again let me fly."

Crystallized Steps
Inspired by Surfer's Path- Jupiter Beach Park by Ted Matz

You and your fragile steps, careful not to break.
Although you crush mountains with your voice,
your steps remain light, mindful of ears.

When you trample cities, you salvage hearts.
Unknowing of what lies past the rose quartz trap,
set to match your soul, you continue.

Guide me through the lilac trees
and pay no mind to the shadow
that impersonates me. When we arrive,

I too, will embody the blithe shade you've established.

The Ghost on The Water
    -Inspired by Matthew 14:22-36

Why do I cover my eyes while at the helm of my ship?

The heavy clouds collect over me, applauding their arrival,
marching through the wind. The drunken current takes me.

How could I find the way to shore, if I crack my compass?
Letting it slip into the space where possibilities drown.

I cannot steer. On an empty vessel I clamor,
"Someone, take my place!"

Through the crowding mist you loosen my grip,
releasing my eyes. Waves like stalagmites tower
from every vantage, but my eyes are now open.

Looking Down from a Cloud

Despair rises in debris
and forms shadows around
me, hovering over tombstones

where my peace lies.
Floating past possibilities
of a brighter perspective,

I look over the edge.
The turn of
tormenting tendencies

drip me into a subtle torrent.
I take my plunge into
the burden of judgement.

When the Beach Aligns with Us

The toasting embrace of the
sky we shared keeps the
cold truth away.

Seashells like stars,
and rested views of beaches
speak for constellations we named
while laying on our backs.

Jumping into waves,
crawling out, drenched in spontaneity.
Heavy denim could not weigh
down the joys in adventurous pursuits.

An afternoon rendezvous, where
we'd elope to salted heavens.

Bargaining In My Sleep

I look for memories already engraved
in the backs of our minds.
Regret overwhelms me,
fools me in my deep sleep.

I inhale the Sandman's dust,
tasting peace and sanity.

Last words became hallucinations of promises.
Last words would turn to agreements
and compromises.

If it had gone like a dream,
you'd believe in me again.

Filter

Hazed hope being blurred
by a blue lens, provide my inability
to find shades of living sun.

The sky has dropped
and invaded my perception.
Clouds clog my lungs,

I exhale puffs of debris.
Broken parts put in place
of what should be mint.

I exert fragmented desires
mixed with kaleidoscope heaves
of polluted atmosphere.

Corrupted will faces
the unyielding restraint:
a gas mask in the clouds.

That of which is involuntarily
stuck to me, keeping me from
taking deep breathes.

In the Letter I Wrote to You

Dreaming of star clusters that fade
into shades of rose dust,
I think of you: the girl that reminds me

of peace. She rides on waves of shy skies.
Soft skin flows in the light
of early morning mist.

Subtle kindness wins my trust.
I melt into the sand beside you,
two silhouettes outlined by the

prying moonlight. The waves subside
into a rhythm that accompanies
the melody in your voice.

I used to hear the music of new hope.
You sang courage into scared bones,
and I danced back to life, praying—
wishing that you would join me.

Long Nights

> *"First you take a drink,*
> *then the drink takes a drink,*
> *then the drink takes you."* —F. Scott Fitzgerald

Beyond performing lights are
silent eyes radiating drunken fools.
Bulbs of translucent ambrosia
leak through shut doors.

Puffs of corrupted hopes
lead mischief to success
and logic to treason.
Bright sounds of tainted affairs

(the bane that pours from veins
of passion) and ascending crowds
of glorious oddities, from a bottle,
drain out life into wonders.

Flooded realities spill
on stubborn souls,
deluged dreams descend
down, drowning them.

Engraved Backs

The treasure that I fight for
is greater than that of the sky.
The jewels that hang
deserve a new finish.

The cracks in my back,
where you've hidden,
collected dust in your absence.
Birthmarks to testify life.

I rose to shield you from
the falling stars. These crystals
lost their will to shoot.

You still marvel at them,
through the holes they've
cut in me.

I will be the diamond-cut distraction.

How to Not Wake Up

The clicking of the blinds
from the breeze
through an open window
snap my eyelids back.

I hear the empty stomach
of the mechanical jungle:
engines growling through the street.

Drowning in my sheets,
I hold my breath desperately
trying to drift
into the unconscious state.

When the Sun finds me
I am hiding under Mount Comforter,
a mountain range to shiver the Alps.

How do I embrace the day?

I broaden the distance still.

All seeing light, I sleep in your shadow.
A routine I know well, bent to disobey.

This Identity

If I begin to list my regrets
I'd slip into new clothes
and have to take on a second name.

You could call me Pathetic,
but I won't be able to respond.
I'll be too busy choking back
mistakes from past lives.

Born into old jeans and tattered shirts
my name held inevitable miseries.
So, each time you called out to me,
my shoulders hung lower
and the color in my clothes faded.

I'll rip this ancestral line
from each thread stitched into me.

"Hello? Anybody There?"

Like yelling into caves and mountain ranges
to see which ones echo back,
I'll lose my voice in doing so.

A loss of will in my letters to God.

Worse than, "Lost in Transit",
they are marked, "Return To Sender".
The evidence that you've read them!

But my pleas come back alphabet soup:
tough to decipher.

I find myself looking for instruction
in spoonfuls. Matching letters together,
but there are so many beneath the surface.

In my hunger I've eaten postage.

Coming to Terms with Letting Go

I did not fight for you,
although I contended
a million disputes in my head

and bargained my way through grief.
I did not fight for you.
Instead, I chose to wrestle

with poisonous habits.
The days are longer,
the nights darker.

But as they pass,
I rehearse acceptance.
Face to face with change,
I am cyclically frightened.

Looking Back on Second Chances

Secrets linger letting thoughts act as pests.
Dinner dates and inside jokes become
hidden languages disguised as casual looks.

I have collected paintings forged by
the fading image of you.
You've picked up new habits,
but still, the same passion.

In hope, I strive for a new love
to give you. So, you remember me,
associate me with pure efforts
and good intentions.

Portioned Kisses

You have sipped from my suffering, in doses.
One teaspoon for each discrepancy,
the ones of sterling silver with the Meadow Rose handle.

Making sure to leave no trace, you melt them
into my skin when you're done.

With ten remaining in your collection, greed grows.
Frame me gluttonous. I am overfed,
while you savor crumbs on glass plates.

Florida's Skin

The sun has laid to rest on the still night.
Mice scurry home and ants follow.
Raccoons attempt to steal the night,
but this full moon beat them to it.
Kin of the little dipper
tarnish a clean get-away.

Water droplets mope in the air,
they gather for comfort.
A longing lingers in the atmosphere-
footprints of heavy breathing.

Fallen twigs, and pebbles
gather around summer moss.
Romantic mother nature,
tracing love by the bonfire.

Frozen in the Past

Memories, like snow, are slow to fade,
but still I visit every night.

And until my jaw is frozen shut
I will dive head first into the absence.

The moments trapped
behind my eyes mimic snowflakes:

failing to materialize
for commemoration.

My useless mind only serves
to ruminate around regret.

An uncontrollable
subconscious drags me

through days that have long gone.
The past collects in an avalanche

rushing down, leaving me
to echo on this peak.

Lissette Lendeborg is originally from the Dominican Republic, although moved to Miami, Florida at a young age, she continues to connect to her roots. Growing up in Miami, Lissette found the need for a strong sense of identity and was able to find that through her faith. From a young age, credited, in part, to her faith, she began focusing on fulfilling a greater purpose. Lissette started writing creatively, the moment she could hold a pencil. She was drawn to storytelling and figurative language; she had found her purpose. She began researching ways to develop this talent, when she found an arts school in the Wynwood area. Once enrolled into the Creative Writing program, she knew there was nothing else she wanted to do. Lissette was able to spend her high school years writing and submitting work to countless publications, contests, and events. She has been awarded a Gold Key by Scholastics Art and Writing on the regional level, and a Silver Key at the national level. After many denials and edits, Lissette is proud to say she has poetry published by *Poetry Matters, Orange Island Review*, and *Di-Verse-City Youth Anthology*; which have been accumulated over her years in high school. She has been invited to read her work at the Miami Book Fair on two separate occasions. In 2017, she was awarded the Playwright Discovery Award by the John F. Kennedy Center of the Performing Arts. Her prose writing can be found published by Litro Magazine. Having spent years training in more classical forms of Creative Writing, Lissette is now spending time establishing her screenwriting and directing skills. Since high school, Lissette has attempted studying Creative Writing at Purdue University, but was unable to find a reason to stay. Looking for more of a learning opportunity, she moved to Los Angeles where she took classes at the Upright Citizens Brigade and the Writing Pad. Back in Miami, she is now studying at the New York Film Academy, developing her eye in film. At only nineteen years old she has the honor of her first full collection of poems being published. She now spends time writing, and training Brazilian Jiu Jitsu, her only other passion. Lissette looks forward to a bright future.

www.ingramcontent.com/pod-product-compliance
Lightning Source LLC
LaVergne TN
LVHW041520070426
835507LV00012B/1699